François Guizot

Love in Marriage

A historical study

François Guizot

Love in Marriage
A historical study

ISBN/EAN: 9783337110857

Printed in Europe, USA, Canada, Australia, Japan

Cover: Foto ©ninafisch / pixelio.de

More available books at **www.hansebooks.com**

LOVE IN MARRIAGE.

An Historical Study.

LADY RACHAEL RUSSELL.

By GUIZOT.

TRANSLATED FROM THE FRENCH BY
MARGUERITE O. STEVENS.

New York:
PUBLISHED BY CARLTON & PORTER,
200 MULBERRY-STREET.
1865.

Entered according to Act of Congress, in the year 1864,

By CARLTON & PORTER,

in the Clerk's Office of the District Court of the United States for the Southern District of New-York.

PREFACE.

THE translator of this brochure was in Paris about the time that it appeared from the press. It produced no little excitement among the Parisian reading public. The name of Guizot was, of course, a guarantee that it was worthy of attention; its title, however, presented greater attractions. "L'Amour Dans le Mariage" is a phrase of peculiarly doubtful significance to the fashionable and literary society of the French metropolis, in which the great author holds a pre-eminent place. Curiosity was awakened to ascertain what he could say on a subject deemed so ambiguous. Had he, like his distinguished cotemporaries, Cousin and Michelet, tired of the philosophy of History, and undertaken to refresh his old age by the study of sentiment and romance? Thousands, attracted by the title of the little book, were doubtless disappointed; but all of elevated taste must have been favorably undeceived. The veteran writer had delineated, in his severest historic style, an example, in noble life, of the purest moral nobleness, a romance of reality, full of human tenderness and religious beauty. He had no need of the aids of meretricious sentimentality or embellishment. The cutting of the diamond must follow the cleavage of its own natural facets.

On returning to America with her manuscript, the translator noticed in the newspapers the announcement of a version by one of our most celebrated female authors. The manuscript was therefore thrown aside; but the advertised translation failed to appear. It was probably found inconvenient to obtain in this country some of the English letters used in French by Guizot, and obviously a retranslation from the French into English would be inadmissible in documents requiring verbal exactness. The present translator has the advantage of possessing these letters.

Guizot has not only presented in these pages a beautiful example of "Love in Marriage," but has illuminated one of the most interesting passages of British history.

CONTENTS.

		PAGE
I.	ROMANCE AND FACT	9
II.	LORD SOUTHAMPTON	12
III.	THE FAMILY OF RUVIGNY	24
IV.	YOUTH OF LADY RUSSELL	32
V.	LORD WILLIAM RUSSELL	37
VI.	LOVE IN MARRIAGE	44
VII.	TRIAL AND EXECUTION OF LORD RUSSELL	54
VIII.	LADY RUSSELL IN WIDOWHOOD	82
IX.	HER LATTER YEARS	114
X.	HER LAST DAYS	131

LOVE IN MARRIAGE.

I

Romance and Fact.

The demand of the present day is for romances. But why do we not search history for them? There human life is found in its most varied and dramatic scenes; there the human heart is displayed with its most vivid passions, with the sovereign charm of variety over all. I admire and enjoy imagination as much as any one; that creative power which draws existences from nothing, animates them, colors them, and makes them live before us, revealing the resources of the soul through all the vicissitudes of destiny. But characters who have really lived, who have truly experienced adverse fortunes and the passions, joys, and griefs which have such an influence over us, when I see these closely and intimately, they attract and retain my interest much more powerfully than the most perfect poem or romance. When the divine traits of that work of God, the living being, are shown to us, it is more beautiful to me than any human creation; for of all poets God is the greatest.

In studying the history of England I have found two narratives more interesting, in my opinion, than any romance. The first is that of a king making a marriage of affection, and the other the devoted attachment in domestic life of a great, liberal, and Christian nobleman. The privacy of the family is unvailed, revealing its sweetest and most charming secrets; while the real actors are the loftiest characters of the empire, and the scenes are amid the grandest events of public life. I may, perhaps, at some future time refer to the royal marriage; but it is the household of the nobleman I wish now to present to my readers.

II.

Lord Southampton.

ONE of the most independent, and at the same time one of the most faithful of the counselors and defenders of Charles the First in his adversities, was Thomas Wriothesley, Earl of Southampton. He had naturally no taste for courtly life or power, or personal grandeur. The almost simultaneous death of his father and eldest brother suddenly put him in possession of the fortune and title of his family; but he was more embarrassed than pleased with his newly-acquired honors, and for some time, it is said, he blushed and turned aside his head whenever he was addressed as "My Lord." He was naturally melancholy, inactive, and proud, full of sensibility, but reserved and silent, though strongly attached to his own ideas and sentiments, and ready to sacrifice everything for them. Perhaps he was somewhat proudly defiant to those who opposed them, but he was without ambition or desire for domination, seldom hopeful or sanguine of success, and never left his retirement except at the call of duty or necessity. When the debate between Charles I. and the Long Parliament commenced, Lord Southampton took his place in the House of Lords with very unfavorable feelings toward the pretensions of the crown and its ministers, and particularly toward Lord Stafford. As a good Englishman he wished to respect the laws, national traditions, and the intervention of Parliament in the affairs of his country. If he did not consider liberty of conscience an inalienable right, like a good and upright

Christian he was displeased with any tyranny attempted in these matters, and he desired more tolerance and charity toward those who differed from him in opinion. In the early days of the Long Parliament he often voted against the bishops and the crown for the reform of abuses, or the punishment of violent despotism, both religious and political. He seldom appeared at court, and began to be regarded by the king as a malcontent, like his friend the Earl of Essex. When, however, popular violence broke forth, when the disorders of the iniquitous Parliament could no longer be concealed, when he saw the laws violated and the monarchy menaced by new despots, he suddenly returned and took his place, without eagerness or confidence, but with a proud conscientiousness, among the defenders or rather servants of the king.

Though a stranger to all party combinations or systematic plans, and without any intention of reforming the constitution of his country in the future, he opposed injustice, illegality, disorder, and violence in the present, not troubling himself about abstract principles, or the distant hopes which they might have held forth to others. The proceedings of Parliament against Lord Stafford appeared to him arbitrary, and his punishment undeservedly severe; and he defended him, though he had at first attacked him. Both Houses had voted that it was inexpedient for any of their members to give themselves to the personal service of the Crown; he accepted, though with regret, the office of privy counselor to the king, and afterward that of gentleman of the bed-chamber. When civil war broke out, though he detested the measure, and had no hopes of a happy settlement whichever party should be successful, he immediately took his place in the royal army, was at the battle of Edgehill, and though he was every day more dissatisfied with the court, followed it to Oxford, maintaining in its midst all his independence and proud susceptibility. One day in the council he expressed himself in severe terms against Prince Rupert and his arrogance toward the English nobility. The prince, to whom the statements were reported with the usual amount of exaggeration, inquired of him if they were true. The earl acknowledged and maintained his opinion by an exact repetition of his words. Prince Rupert, deeply offended by his remarks, informed him that he should be ready to receive satisfaction from him in a sword encounter on horseback. They met the next day.

"What weapons do you choose?" asked the prince.

"I have," said the earl, "no horse here suitable for this service; I do not know where to find one immediately; besides, I am too small and too feeble to measure myself thus with your highness. I beg you to excuse me, and allow me to use the weapons to which I am accustomed. I will fight with pistols on foot."

Prince Rupert unhesitatingly accepted. The seconds were chosen, and the rendezvous was fixed for the next day; but the affair got abroad. The Lords of the Council interfered, closed the gates of the city, summoned witnesses, and succeeded in reconciling the earl with the prince, who treated him afterward with the greatest regard.

When the war terminated, and the king fell into the power of Parliament, Lord

Southampton eagerly sought every opportunity of approaching him, and every means of serving him. When all efforts had failed, when the trial, condemnation, and execution of Charles left nothing more to be hoped or attempted, he did not consider himself released from his duty to his king. The 18th of February, 1649, the day when the royal remains were to be buried in Windsor Castle, Lord Southampton was present to accompany to the tomb the coffin of the prince whom he had neither been able to save nor enlighten. The snow fell in abundance, and in its short passage the black velvet pall that covered the bier was completely white with it, an emblem of the innocence which his faithful followers hoped to prove of him who was beneath it.

After the abolition of royalty, while the Republic and Cromwell were in power,

Lord Southampton lived retired in his castle, at Tichfield, in Hampshire, as much a stranger to the plots of his party as to the new rulers of his country. Inflexibly faithful to the proscribed Charles II., he transmitted not only useful advice to him, but all the money he could raise on his fortune, though it had been much reduced by sequestration and taxes. But he took no more decisive part with the insurrectionary attempts of the royalists, nor with the malcontent republicans, nor in intriguing alliances with foreigners. His good sense, his zealous patriotism, and his natural indolence, all conspired to retain him in this attitude of honorable inactivity. One day he learned that Cromwell, who had come into Hampshire on the occasion of the marriage of his son Richard, had mentioned his intention of surprising him with a visit. Lord Southampton immediately left his castle, and returned to it only when Cromwell had left the county.

After the Restoration, notwithstanding his previous inactivity, Lord Southampton found himself in the first rank of the lords and former counselors of Charles I., whom the royalist opinions now called into power. He was also the intimate friend of Chancellor Hyde, who was on the most confidential terms with Charles II. He was Grand Treasurer at the same time that Hyde became Lord Chancellor and Earl of Clarendon. During seven years the two friends, one in principle, though very different in character, exerted themselves to sustain at the same time the heartless and corrupt monarch, the discontented, though triumphant party, and the austere, humiliated, and irritated nation. Clarendon, who was ambitious, laborious, and passionate for his Church, his cause, his power, and his rank, struggled strenuously against his former and later enemies, and against the decline of his favor with his royal pupil, who had become his king. Southampton, who was less active, preferring his ease and leisure, was also of a more liberal mind and heart; tormented besides by disease, he discharged his duties conscientiously, and made vain efforts to maintain order and probity in the finances of the Crown; was often sad, disgusted, sick, and frequently manifested, to Clarendon's great vexation, his desire of retiring from a situation which he occupied without pleasure and without success.

In the last century France also possessed two men of rare virtue and of somewhat similar character, Turgot and Malesherbes, who were associated together in the exercise of power. Turgot was full of ardor, faith, hope, and perseverance. Malesherbes was as sincere, but more feeble; more easily discouraged, often saying, "Turgot does not wish me to resign; he does not see that we shall both be driven from our positions." They were, in fact, both dismissed by a king, good-hearted like themselves, who valued them, but who defended them no better than he defended himself. Charles II., who was as clear-sighted as he was corrupt, soon perceived Lord Southampton's reluctance for his position, resolved to take advantage of it, and rid himself noiselessly from an inconveniently independent counselor; but Clarendon exerted all his remaining credit to continue his friend in office, as he had continued himself, and Lord Southampton remained Grand Treasurer till his death, which happened a few months after. He bade adieu to his position and to life without bowing, like the Lord Chancellor in the sadness of exile, under the unjust hatred of the people and the ingratitude of the king.

III.

The Family of Ruvigny.

Lord Southampton had married Rachael de Ruvigny, a French lady, a descendant of one of those noble families* who, in the sixteenth century, had embraced the cause of the Reformation, though feeble and persecuted from its cradle. Faith and conscience had induced them to take this course, for no personal interest and no temptation of riches or power had influenced them. At the time of the marriage of Lord Southampton with Rachael de Ruvigny the edict of Nantes was in

---

* Their name was Massue, seigneurs of Raynevel, in Picardy, Marquis de Ruvigny. *Vide* "Dictionnaire de la Noblesse de la Chesnaye des Bois," tome ix, p. 594; and "Nobilliare de Picardie."

full vigor, and Richelieu, though persecuting and destroying the Protestants as a political party, left their religious rights undisturbed, and even employed without hesitation in various public positions those among them whom he found devoted to the interest of the Crown and to himself. Mazarin followed the example of Richelieu; he was as wise in the recognition of the religious liberty of the Protestants, but more timid in admitting them to the offices of State. Though free and tranquil within the limits of the edict, conquered Protestantism lost daily in France that real strength of action and of general opinion which are the only sure guarantee of liberty. Protestant churches were not closed, and the Protestants were not driven from their country; but they were repulsed in private life, and made to feel the isolation of foreigners. The brother of Lady Southampton, the Marquis de Ruvigny, was one of the most able and important Protestants of that period. During the troubles of the Fronde, he gave to Anne of Austria and to Mazarin himself proofs of active, useful, and persevering fidelity. With the reduction of the Fronde, Mazarin, wishing to reward Ruvigny, chose him as Deputy-General of the National Synod of the Reformed Churches of France. The office comprised a double function, making him *Chargé d'Affaires* from the king to the Protestants, and from the Protestants to the king. Ruvigny discharged this delicate mission with skillful zeal; though often disliked, and even suspected by both parties, he remained equally faithful to the king and to his own Church, and was little disturbed by their alternate displeasure if he but succeeded in maintaining peace and right between them. The office, however, was not one which pleased him, and he had other hopes for his ambition. He wished to open a different career for himself, either in the army or out of it; but he was soon given to understand that no such opportunity as he desired could be expected without a change of religion. He was appointed to some services with the Protestants which he alone could manage, but beyond this the future was utterly closed to him.

After the death of Mazarin and the restoration of the Stuarts, the numerous relatives of Ruvigny in England, his intimate connections with the Southampton, Russell, and other important families, both in the court and opposition, readily obtained for him, without efforts on his part, that which he had formerly vainly desired. He was employed in various secret negotiations between the courts of Paris and London, now laboring to produce harmony between the two kings, and now to secure the influence of Louis XIV. over the most ardent leaders of the opposition in Parliament. The French monarch had a sincere esteem for him, and Charles II. treated him with marked favor: "I have told Ruvigny all that is my heart. . . . France has never gone so far in its manifestation of good intentions as when he resided here," Charles wrote to his sister, the Duchess of Orleans. As a good Frenchman, a devoted royalist, and a sincere Protestant, Ruvigny made great efforts to serve his country, his king, and his religion at the same time, without any illusive hopes, however, of more than a brief success in this difficult attempt. The Edict of Nantes yet existed, but like a ruined and abandoned edifice, which only awaits one decided blow to lay it in ruins. Under the impulse of the general sentiment of catholic France, and at the pressing intercession of the clergy, Louis XIV., led on by that false and fatal idea that civil power has a right over conscience, and that unity of state is identified with unity of faith, with a want of probity which he would not have been guilty of toward foreigners, broke, sometimes secretly and sometimes openly, the royal promises and legal guaranties which a part of his own subjects had received from his ancestors. The Marquis de Ruvigny, though a faithful servant of the king, could not blind himself to the final issue of this proceeding; resolving when the last moment should come to sacrifice everything rather than his faith and the honor of his soul, he took care to secure for himself and his children letters of naturalization in Eugland, and in January, 1680, he wrote to his niece, Lady Russell: "I send you our letters of naturalization, which will be safer in your hands than in mine. I beg you and also your sister (Lady Elizabeth Noel) to preserve them for me. They may be of service, for nothing is more uncertain than events." Events were not, however, long uncertain. Five years afterward the Edict of Nantes was formally revoked. With great difficulty Ruvigny obtained, through the personal favor of Louis XIV. as a reward for his services, the privilege of exiling himself and his family from his country, instead of making a precipitate flight. Some years later, in 1711, the king gave to the Abbe de Polignac the confiscation of the property of his son, Henry de Ruvigny, who had then become Lord Galway, in the service of William III. of England.

Aside from its general consequences, the revocation of the Edict of Nantes cost France and the king three excellent and glorious servants: the Marshal de Schomberg in the army, Admiral Duquesne in the navy, and the Marquis de Ruvigny in diplomacy.

IV.

Youth of Lady Russell.

From the marriage of the Earl of Southampton with Rachael de Ruvigny a daughter was born in 1636, who bore like her mother the name of Rachael. The offspring of this noble and conscientious pair was educated in the English and French traditions of virtue and piety; she received, besides, from the events in which her youth was passed, those strong moral impressions which never fail to elevate souls who are not crushed beneath their weight. She early learned to sympathize deeply with the misfortunes of others, and to endure domestic afflictions patiently. Her mother died during her infancy, and Lord Southampton married a second time, an occasion naturally of much domestic annoyance, even when it is not the source of real troubles; but he preserved the tenderest affection for the two daughters of his first wife, and Rachael fondly loved and respected her father. She saw him, without sanguine illusions or mental servility, devoted to that political party which, after due consideration, he believed the most just, remaining at the same time a royalist and a patriot. The actions and conversation of Lord Southampton were marked by an enlightened but firm piety. In the life which his daughter led, nothing could trouble or destroy the salutary impressions which these examples had produced upon her character. At the time when she passed from childhood to youth she lived far from the world, in the country, in those habits of tranquillity, dignity, and simplicity, social elevation and popular benevolence, which are the best honor of a Christian aristocracy. In 1653, at seventeen years of age, she was beautiful, pious, and vivacious, without excess or want of imagination, disposed to enjoy life peaceably, receiving benefits as mercies, and adversities as lessons from the hand of God. At this time Lord Vaughan, eldest son of the Earl of Carbury, asked her hand in marriage, according to previous arrangements, which had been made by the relatives almost without her knowledge. Speaking afterward of this marriage to one of her friends, she said it was one of those unions which was rather accepted than chosen by either party. She went to reside with her father-in-law at Golden Grove, in Wales, and fulfilled all the duties of her new situation without effort or pretension, inspiring the liveliest affection in all around her, but producing no other effect than those naturally resulting from her gentle virtues, her agreeable disposition, and her perfect and constant kindness, which was remarked by every one. "There is no charm in the world comparable with kindness," wrote one of her husband's friends to her, "and you are the best proof of it. All who know you are compelled to honor you; and you owe them no gratitude for it, for they cannot do otherwise." Fourteen years thus flowed on in virtuous and modest happiness. In 1665, the only child of this marriage was born, but it scarcely survived its birth. We have no particulars of her husband's death, but in 1667 she was a widow, and resided with her beloved sister, Lady Elizabeth Noel, in the castle of their father, where their infancy had been spent. At

Lord Southampton's death he left all his fortune to his two daughters. Tichfield became the inheritance of Lady Noel; and the grounds and castle of Stratton, situated also in Hampshire, fell to Lady Vaughan.

V.

Lord William Russell.

About the same time William Russell, the second son of the Earl of Bedford, a young man, three years younger than Lady Vaughan, made his *début* in society and in public life. After three years of travel upon the continent he returned to England, a short period before the Restoration, and was elected a member of the House of Commons which placed Charles II. upon the throne. Scarcely any traces remain of his life and character at that time. A note from him to Mr. Thornton indicates a sincerely pious disposition. "I am recovered," he wrote, "of an unruly sickness which brought me so low that I was just at death's door: my prayers to God are to give me, together with my health, grace to employ it in his service, and to make good use of this visitation by the serious application of it." The manners of the time, however, the example of the Court, and the impetuosity of youth, sometimes betrayed him into irregularities of life. He was engaged in several duels, excited probably by trivial causes; but at the moment of this always solemn act, however frivolous the occasion, serious sentiments reappeared in the soul of young William Russell, which was impressed with an affectionate simplicity and touching kindness. The second of July, 1663, he wrote to his father, the Earl of Bedford:

"My Lord: Although I think I have courage enough to fight with anybody without despairing of the victory, yet nevertheless knowing that the issue of combats depends upon fortune, and that it is not always he that has most courage and the justest cause who overcomes, but he that is luckiest; and having found myself very unlucky in several things, I have thought fit to leave these few lines behind me to express (in case I should miscarry) some kind of acknowledgment for the goodness your lordship has had in showing me so much kindness above what I have deserved. I have the deepest sense of it in the world, and shall always (during life) make it my business to express it by my life and actions. For really, my lord, I think myself the happiest man in the world in a father, and I hope (if I have not already) I should, at least for the future, have carried myself so as not to make your lordship think yourself unhappy in a son. My lord, in case I miscarry, (for without it I suppose this will not come to your hands,) let me beg of you to remember me in the persons of those who have served me well. Pray, let not my friend Taaffe suffer for his generous readiness to serve me, not only on this occasion, but in several others wherein he has showed himself a very generous and kind friend to me; therefore, pray bring him off clear, and let him not suffer for my sake. For my men, I doubt not your lordship will reward them well. For Robin, my footman, because he has served me faithfully, carefully, and with great affection, I desire that twenty pounds a year may be settled on him during his life; and the Frenchman I hope you will reward very well, having served with care and affection. For my debts, I hope your lordship will see them paid, and therefore I shall set them down to prevent mistakes. I owe one hundred pounds, forty pounds, and, I think, some four or five more to my Lord Brook. This is all I owe which I can call to mind at present, except for the clothes and some other things I have had this winter, of which my man can give an account. I have not time to write any longer, therefore I shall conclude with assuring your lordship that I am, as much as it is possible for me to be, my lord, your lordship's most dutiful son and humble servant, WILLIAM RUSSELL."

With such a respectful, tender soul life could not always be disorderly. It was not long before his conduct rose to the level of his moral nature. Lady Vaughan was probably not a stranger to the re-establishment of moral harmony in the noble young man to whom she soon gave herself. Of all human influences that of virtuous love is the sweetest, as it is the most powerful. No details remain of their first acquaintance; it is only known, by a letter from Lady Percy, the half sister of Lady Vaughan, that in 1667 William Russell was charmed with the beautiful widow. "He manifests," she writes, "like many others, an ardent desire to gain the heart, which is such a desirable conquest to all." Lady Vaughan was a rich heiress, without children from her first marriage. William Russell, who was a younger son, had neither title nor fortune to offer her. He was undoubtedly on this account more timid and reserved; but there was too much innate and intimate sympathy between them to allow worldly considerations long to separate them. The marriage took place in the beginning of the year 1670, but, according to the usage of English society, the bride retained her title of Lady Vaughan till 1678, when, by the death of his elder brother, William Russell became the heir of his house, and took the title of Lord Russell. We have good reason to suppose that if Lady Vaughan had lived in our time, she would not have waited so long before adopting the name of the man she loved. Personal feelings have conquered aristocratic taste in this respect; and more recently Lady Cowper did not hesitate, in her marriage with Lord Palmerston, to renounce her own title for the name and inferior title of her husband.

VI.

Love in Marriage.

This world has nothing to offer more charming than the example of a pure and happy affection. That full and sincere outburst of the interior strength and desires of the soul, which we call Love, has such a charm for us that we contemplate it with the profoundest interest, even when we find it mingled with culpable errors, troubles, discontent, and grief; but when it is seen in harmony with conscience, filling the soul with joy, leaving its beauty and peace unchanged, it is the richest treasure of our nature; it is the most human, and at the same time the most divine, gratification of our aspirations; it is Paradise regained.

The union of Rachael Wriothesley and William Russell presented this rare and beautiful character. Hitherto Rachael has appeared tranquil, simple, unpretending, and virtuous, pursuing modestly the strict but ordinary routine of life. But now passionate love and supreme happiness have taken unsought possession of that heart so well constituted to enjoy them; she gives herself up to her new felicity with full liberty and confidence; she loves as ardently as innocently, and she is perfectly happy. "If I were more fortunate in my expression," she writes to her husband, "I could do myself more right when I would own to my dearest Mr. Russell what real and perfect happiness I enjoy from that kindness he allows me every day to receive new marks of, such as, in spite of the knowledge I have of my own wants, will not suffer me to mistrust I want his love, though I do to merit so desirable a blessing; but my best life, you that know so well how to love and to oblige, make my felicity entire, by believing my heart possessed with all the gratitude, honor, and passionate affection to your person any creature is capable of, or can be obliged to." And elsewhere, eight years after: "My dearest heart, flesh and blood cannot have a truer and greater sense of their own happiness than your poor but honest wife has. I am glad you find Stratton so sweet; may you live to do so one fifty years more; and if God pleases I shall be glad I may keep your company most of those years, unless you wish other at any time; then I think I could willingly leave all in the world, knowing you would take care of our brats; they are both well, and your great one's letter she hopes came to you."

And yet again, a year later: "To see anybody preparing and taking their leave to see what I long to do a thousand times more than they, makes me not endure to suffer their going, without saying something to my best life, though it is a kind of anticipating my joy when we shall meet, to allow myself so much before the time . . . I would fain be telling my heart more things—anything to be in a kind of talk with him, but I believe Spencer stays for my dispatch. He was willing to go early; but this was to be the delight of the morning and the support of the day. 'Tis written in bed, thy pillow at my back, where thy dear head shall lie, I hope, to-morrow night, and many more, I trust in His mercy, notwithstanding all our enemies or ill-wishers. Love, and be willing to be loved by," etc.

Lady Russell did not limit herself to

expressions of love to her husband; she manifested it actively in smaller as well as in more important things, in her associations with his relatives, in conforming to all his tastes, living with him in society when he wished it, and in the country when he preferred that, and in taking care of his amusement as well as his happiness. When they were separated, one at London and the other at Stratton, as seldom happened, however, she collected all the news, political as well as social, all that related to the affairs of their friends, or the incidents of society; communicating everything to him promptly and simply, without any attempt at displaying her abilities, but only her desire to interest or divert him by all the means in her power. "I am very sure my dearest Mr. Russell meant to oblige me extremely when he enjoined me to scribble to him by the post, as knowing he could not do a kinder thing than to let me see he designed not to think me impertinent in it; though we parted but this morning, which I might reasonably have doubted to have been, when I have passed all this long day and learned nothing new can entertain you and your good company. All I see either are, or appear, duller than when you are here; and I do not find the town is enlivened by the victory we have obtained.* There is no more talked of than you heard last night, nor anything printed, because no letters have come yet. Lord Howard's son is expected every hour with them. Many whisper the French behaved themselves not like firm friends. The Duke of York's marriage is broken off. That or

* The naval battle of Tolbay, of the 26th of May, 1672, in which the Duke of York, sustained by a French squadron, gained a dear-bought advantage over the Dutch fleet commanded by De Ruyter.

other cause makes him look less in good humor than ordinary. They say she is offered the king of Spain, and our prince shall have D'Elbœuf," etc.

Besides, and shall I say above, this love so deep and tender, there was, I will not say another love, because I do not like the use of similar terms to express emotions so widely different; there was, however, another sentiment which filled the soul of Lady Russell, strengthening her during her days of happiness for the day of trial. She was a Christian, a true Christian in mind and in heart, full of faith in Christian doctrines and submission to Christian precepts. She had no sectarian spirit, no taste for religious disputation, and toward those who differed from her she showed an elevated and intelligent charity. We shall see when God proved her, with what rare prudence and beautiful harmony her

Christian sentiments and her earthly affections, her love and her piety, were reconciled. The reader will not fail to remark the power of faith in her soul, preparing her with a strong but humble trust, while she was perfectly contented and happy with her earthly lot, to accept from the hand of God the blows, or rather the blow, of which she sometimes seemed to have a presentiment. In one of those letters to her husband, in which she pours out her love in passionate expressions of gratitude and tenderness, she stops herself suddenly and says to him: "What have I to ask but a continuance (if God see fit) of these present enjoyments; if not, a submission without a murmur to his most wise dispensations and unerring providence, having a thankful heart for the years I have been so perfectly contented in. He knows best when we have had enough here: what I most earnestly beg from his mercy is, that we both live so as whichever goes first, the other may not sorrow as for one they have no hope. Then let us cheerfully expect to be together to a good old age; if not, let us not doubt but he will support his servants under what trials he will inflict upon them. These are necessary meditations sometimes, that we may not be surprised above our strength by a sudden accident, being unprepared. Excuse me if I dwell too long upon it. It is firmly my opinion that if we can be prepared for all conditions, we can with the greater tranquillity enjoy the present, which I hope will be long, though when we change it will be for the better I trust, through the merit of Christ. Let us daily pray it may be so, and then admit of no fears. Death is the extremest evil against nature, it is true. Let us overcome the immoderate fear of it, either to our friend or self, and then what light hearts may we live with."

Ten years passed away from the day when Lady Russell addressed these pious words from London to her husband, then at Stratton. Lord Russell was now in his turn at London, and his wife wrote him from Stratton, the 25th of September, 1682: "I know nothing new since you went; but I know as certainly as I live that I have been for twelve years as passionate a lover as ever woman was, and hope to be so one twelve years more; happy still and entirely yours."

VII.

Trial and Execution of Lord Russell.

Scarcely ten months after this letter, filled with so much love, confidence, and happiness, the storm darkened this pure sky; Lord Russell was a prisoner in the Tower of London, summoned to appear at the Assizes of the Old Bailey to answer to the charge of high treason. For several years he had kept his seat in the House of Commons, though he seldom took part, and perhaps felt little interest in the debates. He was young, and absorbed in the ardent pursuits of youth. England gradually exhausted the joys and hopes to which it gave itself at the Restoration. Remembrances of the revolutionary time, and the reaction against its maxims, its acts and its actors, had filled all minds. Charles II. and his Court had fostered this reaction with licentious egotism: encouraging it by their excesses, they at last exhausted it. Their pretensions, their faults, their vices, excited new questions and new passions. The old royalists, the men who had served Charles I. and combated Cromwell, disappeared. New men, and new parties under their protection, entered upon the stage; the party of the Crown and the party of the country became the Tories and the Whigs; successors, but thoroughly transformed successors, of the "Cavaliers and Roundheads." Parliament had become the arena and essential instrument of politics; the royalist Long-Parliament pursued, though execrating it, the work that the revolutionary Long-Parliament had undertaken. The risen monarchy prevailed by the same arms which had caused its overthrow; the king governed the country by Parliament, and Parliament by its own leaders, who had become the counselors of the Crown.

By a coincidence, which cannot be remarked without interest, it was very nearly at the same time in which Lord Russell married Lady Vaughan that he first engaged actively in the party of the country against the Court. Domestic happiness and patriotic passion commenced simultaneously with him. Of a benevolent and generous heart, and of an elevated mind, though with little breadth or penetration, however, and with a character more obstinate than strong, he was easily influenced, governed, or deceived when his inclinations led him. He soon became one of the most zealous opponents of the Court, and the moral ornament as well as the political leader of his party. Always ready to sacrifice himself, for eleven years in the House of Commons he took the defense, and often the initiative of the most extreme measures of the opposition, among others of the bill proposed to exclude the Duke of York, as a Papist, from the succession to the Crown. With his party and with the nation, besides the merit of his devotion to them, he possessed the additional attraction of almost always sharing their prejudices, passions, and blindness. Superior to them all by his virtues, but resembling them in his opinions and sentiments, he became almost immediately the most popular and honored man in the kingdom; and such was the harmony and sympathy between him and the national party, that there was no means of showing him his own errors or those of his old friends, for warnings came from his enemies only, and they were never believed.

Lady Russell alone, notwithstanding her love and her modesty, had some doubts of the propriety and some anxiety respecting the position of her husband, and she expressed them to him with a frankness as firm as it was tender. In politics, as in religion, she shared the belief, the sentiments, and the wishes of Lord Russell; she had, like him, a lofty and patriotic heart, deeply interested in the fate of her country; but her mind was more correct and comprehensive, less prejudiced, and more penetrating. In March, 1683, when Lord Russell was preparing to sustain a violent opposition motion, he received from his wife, while the House was sitting, this note:

"My sister being here, tells me she overheard you tell her lord last night that you would take notice of the business (you know what I mean) in the House. This alarms me, and I do earnestly beg of you to tell me truly if you have or mean to do it. If you do, I am most assured you will repent it. I beg once more to know the truth. 'Tis more pain to be in doubt, and to your sister too, and if I have any interest, I use it to beg your silence in this case, at least to-day."

It is unnecessary to reread this letter to be convinced that it was not the first time Lady Russell had thus remonstrated with her husband. Her earnestness in conjuring him to tell her the truth contains a gentle reproach that he had often concealed it, and her deep solicitude about what she scarcely dared hope to prevent. Lord Russell was evidently deeply impressed with this entreaty from his wife, for he carefully preserved it, writing with his own hand the date and the place where he had received it. I am inclined to think, however, that he did not follow her advice on this day, nor probably at any other time.

The time at last arrived when the king, though little inclined to political risks, and the Parliament, though monarchical and loyal, could no longer exist together. The national party demanded of Charles II., in the disinheritance of his brother, the destruction of the monarchy with his own hands. The king asked the national party to submit at any risk to a prince who evidently desired the destruction of the religion and constitution of the country. Thus driven to extremity, the king decided to attempt tyranny, and the national party insurrection. At the moment of the crisis, in 1681, when the last Parliament of Charles II. was dissolved, two men, Lord

Shaftesbury and Lord Russell, were at the head of the cabinet. Shaftesbury was already old, and as ambitious and inde fatigable as he was corrupt; he had been perverted by all the influences of corruption, by the Court, power, and popularity. He had exercised himself from his youth in seeking success by plots and intrigues; of an audacious, and yet pliant character; sagacious and fertile in expedients, he was equally skillful in serving or injuring, in pleasing or embroiling. He was attached both by pride and prudence to the Protestant and national party, which appeared to him the strongest, and he was fully determined to save his life in any case—to gather the fruit of his intrigues or to recommence them. Lord Russell was still young, sincere, ardent, and inexperienced; of an upright mind, a heart full of faith and honor, conscientious in all his undertakings, and ready to sacrifice his life for his cause, but incapable of doing anything merely for success. Between these two men, engaged in the same enterprise, but with such different motives, it was easy to foresee which would appear the instrument in case of success, and which the victim if reverses came.

The conspirators, though generally united, were not all of the same opinions, and on account of mutual distrusts their designs were not always known to each other. Lord Russell projected armed resistance to the royal tyranny, and perhaps comprehended the consequences of such a resolution. Lord Shaftesbury clearly saw his design, and, resolved that the king must be overthrown at any price, made arrangements for another successor than the legitimate heir. A sudden attack and the assassination of Charles II. was sometimes proposed; but while some of the Republicans indulged these dreams, others among them were traitors, already bought by the Court, or willing to reveal their secrets and their accomplices to save themselves from peril. At one of their meetings Lord Russell saw Lord Howard, a man whom he despised, enter with Colonel Sidney and Mr. Hampden.

"What have we to do with this rogue?" said he to Lord Essex, his intimate friend, as he rose to withdraw; but Lord Essex, who had a better opinion of Lord Howard, detained him, little suspecting that this man's testimony would ruin them both.

Some days later Lord Mordant, an ardent Royalist, who, though he was very far from being a conspirator himself, was well-disposed to Lord Shaftesbury, had an interview with the king's mistress, the

Duchess of Portsmouth, with whom, for his own advancement, he had formed a secret, but very familiar intimacy. It was suddenly announced to them that the king had arrived and had ascended the staircase. The duchess hastily concealed Lord Mordant in an adjoining closet. Curious, and perhaps a little jealous, he looked through the key-hole and soon saw Lord Howard enter; but he conversed with the king in so low a tone that nothing could be distinctly heard. As soon as the visitors of the duchess had departed, the prisoner was set at liberty. He immediately took a hackney-coach and drove in haste to Lord Shaftesbury, whom he informed of what he had seen.

"Are you perfectly certain of this?" asked the earl as he looked steadily at him.

"Perfectly certain," replied Mordant.

"Well, my lord, you are a young man of honor, and cannot wish to deceive me; if this is true, I must depart this evening."

That same night Lord Shaftesbury left his house, and concealed himself beyond London, where the order was given the next day for his arrest. Some days after he embarked at Harwich and fled to Holland, hoping to find with the Prince of Orange an asylum and an avenger. As Lord Chancellor he had encouraged the war with Holland, often repeating, "Carthage must be destroyed." On his arrival in Amsterdam he was obliged to ask permission of the burgomaster to reside there. The magistrate replied: "Carthage, not yet destroyed, willingly receives the Earl of Shaftesbury within its walls."

At the same time that the order had been given for Lord Shaftesbury's arrest, a writ was issued for Lord Russell's appearance before the council. The messenger who bore the order stationed himself before the principal entrance to the house, but the back doors remained unguarded, perhaps designedly. Lord Russell might have escaped; but he refused, saying his flight would be an acknowledgment, and that he had done nothing which should make him fear the justice of his country. He sent Lady Russell in haste, however, to consult his principal friends, who were all of opinion, from the instructions he had sent them, that it would be better for him to remain. At his appearance before the king and council Charles said to him: "We do not suspect you of any design against my person, but I have strong proofs of your plots against my government." After a long examination, Lord Russell was sent to the Tower. As he entered he told Taunton, his servant, that those who had sworn against him would have his life. Taunton expressed the hope that his enemies would not succeed. "They will have it," said Lord Russell; "the devil is let loose."

I do not intend to detail here this great and celebrated trial. I only wish to retrace the private life of Lord and Lady Russell, their personal relations and mutual sentiments in their time of trial, as well as in their happier hours. From the moment of her husband's arrest, Lady Russell consecrated herself, with an ardor as intelligent as it was firm and passionate, to every measure which might be of service to him. During the fifteen days which passed between his arrest and the sentence, she went, and came, and wrote incessantly, collecting instructions, sustaining the courage of alarmed friends, exciting the interest of the indifferent, and seeking all possible means of assistance while his fate was remaining uncertain, and any chance remained for his salvation from the extreme penalty. She was so actively and absolutely identified with Lord Russell in the general opinion, that when he complained that the list of jurors had not been communicated to him, the lord chief justice and the attorney general justified themselves by proving that Lady Russell had been informed respecting them. The evening before the day when he was to appear before the Court of Assizes she wrote to him: "Your friends, believing I can do you some service at your trial, I am extremely willing to try if my resolution will hold out; pray let yours. But it may be the court will not let me; however, do you let me try." On the 13th of July, 1683, the debate opened; the hall was crowded with spectators. "We have no place to sit," said the officers. Lord Russell asked for pen, ink, and paper to take notes; they were given him.

"May I have somebody write, to help my memory?"

"Yes, my lord, any of your servants."

"My wife is here, my lord, to do it."

Lady Russell rose to express her assent, and a thrill of emotion ran through the entire assembly.

"If my lady please to give herself the trouble," said the chief justice; and during the entire debate Lady Russell was by her husband's side, his only secretary and his most vigilant counselor.

The courage and activity of Lady Russell did not fail when the fatal sentence was pronounced. Her soul was one of those whose strength and hope are sustained above all human calculation, by love, duty, and confidence in God. Every effort was made to save the life of Lord Russell. Some of the most powerful men of the court entreated the king earnestly in his favor; they urged that his pardon would impose a debt of gratitude upon a noble family, while his punishment would prove an injury never to be forgotten. It was also due to the daughter of Lord Southampton. Numerous letters were addressed to Lady Russell to inform her of something further to be attempted, or to designate the day, and hour, and place when she might throw herself at the king's feet, who would be unable to refuse her, they believed. The Duke of York was petitioned as well as the king. He listened quietly, but made no reply. The king answered Monmouth hastily: "I would save him, but I cannot without breaking with my brother; say no more;" and to Lord Dartmouth: "All you say is true; but it is as true that if I do not take his life he will soon have mine." Other more questionable means were tried: the Earl of Bedford offered the Duchess of Portsmouth fifty, and it is even said a hundred, thousand pounds sterling for the pardon of his son. Charles replied, "I will not purchase my own and my subjects' blood at so easy a rate." Lady Russell thought that her uncle, the Marquis de Ruvigny, coming expressly from Paris with the approval of Louis XIV., might have some influence with the king.* Ruvigny promised to be in Lon-

---

* Lord John Russell, in his life of his illustrious ancestor, (Life of Lord William Russell, vol. i, p. 14, and vol. ii, p. 76,) considers as very doubtful the statements of the attempts made in the name of Louis XIV. to save the life of Lord Russell, and the letters of Barillon making mention of them, fragments of which are quoted by Dalrymple. Lord Russell's doubts were very natural, for at that time he was not allowed the opportunity of verifying these citations from Dalrymple in our archives of foreign affairs.

don. "I am very impatient, my dear niece, to be with you," he wrote. "The king arrived three days since, and he has had the goodness to consent to my journey." It was even said that he would bear a letter from Louis XIV., requesting Charles to grant a pardon. "I do not wish to prevent the Marquis de Ruvigny from coming here," said Charles to Baril-

I have since examined these papers, and they prove that Barillon was really charged with some messages to Charles II. in favor of Lord Russell, though they were probably not too earnest. In a letter dated July 29th, (19th of July according to the old style, then maintained in England,) 1683, Barillon gives an account of his proceedings to the king: "Yesterday I showed to the king of England a letter from M. de Ruvigny, and I said to him what your majesty had directed on the subject. The prince replied, 'I am very sure that the king, my brother, would not advise me to pardon a man who would have granted me no quarter; I do not wish to prevent M. de Ruvigny from coming here, but Lord Russell's neck will be cut before his arrival. I owe this example to my own safety, and to the good of the state.'"—*Archives of Foreign Affairs of France.*

lon, "but my Lord Russell's head will be off before he arrives." Ruvigny did not go. At the earnest request of his father, his friends, and doubtless also of his wife, Lord Russell consented to write to the king and the Duke of York, asking pardon for himself, and representing "that he had never had the least thought against his majesty's life, nor any design to change the government, acknowledging that he had erred in attending unlawful meetings, and offering to spend the remainder of his life on the continent in whatever place the king should assign, and to meddle no more in the affairs of England." This attempt, which proved useless like all the others, cost Lord Russell a great effort. As he finished his letter to the Duke of York, he said to Dr. Burnet: "This will be printed, and will be selling about the streets as my submission when I am hanged."

One chance still remained, and to many it seemed the most hopeful, though it was indirect and singular. The question of the possible legality or the absolute illegality of all armed resistance to the lawful sovereign was strongly agitating the public mind. The court and patriotic parties were equally anxious to establish a principle by which their acts could be legally sustained; for such is the noble nature of man that reason is a necessity to him; he cannot even have the enjoyment of power if he feels that it is disavowed by justice and truth. The English Church maintained unreservedly the unlawfulness of armed resistance. Two of its most upright and most moderate dignitaries, Drs. Burnet and Tillotson, undertook to obtain Lord Russell's assent to their opinion, hoping to save his life if they could offer this submission to the king. At one time they thought he appeared a little shaken; and Lord Halifax, to whom they related it, said that when he mentioned it to the king he had seemed more touched than with all the previous solicitations. Lord Russell quietly listened to the redoubled efforts of the two theologians. Tillotson wrote him a letter to establish his position of non-resistance on the foundations of the Gospel. Lord Russell took the letter and withdrew to an adjoining apartment; when he returned he said to the dean, "I have read your arguments, and am willing to be convinced, but cannot say that I am. For my part I cannot deny, but I have been of opinion, that a free nation like this might defend their religion and liberties when invaded and taken from them, though under pretense and color of law. If I have sinned in this I hope God will not lay it to my charge, since he knows it was only a sin of ignorance." Burnet persisted in endeavoring to draw further concessions from him. Lord Russell cut short the discussion, saying, "I cannot tell a lie; and if I go further I should lie." He conversed upon the question with his wife, and so far from encouraging any manifestation of weakness, she sadly approved and sustained him in his sincerity. It is even said that she was displeased with Tillotson's persistance in discussing it.

All these measures and all these hopes, however, successively failed. The fatal day approached. "I should wish," said Lord Russell to Dr. Burnet, "that my wife would give over beating every bush, and running hither and thither to save me; but when I consider that it will be some mitigation of her sorrow afterward to reflect that she has left nothing undone,

I acquiesce." When they were together they appeared mutually occupied in strengthening each other; when she left him he followed her with his eyes, and his emotion appeared overpowering; he conquered himslf by a strong effort, and employed his time entirely when alone or with Burnet and Tillotson in meditations, reading, and pious conversation. The 19th of July, when informed that the petition for a reprieve had been rejected, and that the execution was fixed for the next day, he wrote a letter to the king, to be delivered after his death, which closed with these words: "I crave leave to end my days with this sincere protestation, that my heart was ever devoted to that which I thought was your true interest; in which, if I was mistaken, I hope your displeasure against me will end with my life, and that no part of it shall fall on my wife and children; which is the last petition will ever be offered from, may it please your majesty, your majesty's most faithful, most dutiful, and most obedient subject." The next day, the 20th, he received the sacrament from Tillotson.

"Do you believe all the articles of the Christian religion as taught by the Church of England?" asked the dean.

"Yes, truly."

"Do you forgive all persons?"

"I do, from my heart."

After dinner he re-read and signed the paper which he intended to deliver to the sheriff on the scaffold, as his farewell to his life and his country, and gave Lady Russell all necessary directions for its publication and circulation. Lady Russell then left him to return with his children. He kept them some time, conversed with her respecting their education and their future, embraced them, blessed them, and sent them away without any disturbance of his serenity. "Stay and sup with me," he said to his wife; "let us take our last earthly food together." During supper and afterward he spoke particularly of his two daughters, and also of those great examples in which death was met with calmness and triumph of soul. Toward ten o'clock he rose, took Lady Russell by the hand, embraced her four or five times, while both remained silent and trembling, their eyes filled with tears, which did not fall. She departed. "Now," said Lord Russell to Burnet, the bitterness of death is past;" and abandoning himself to his emotions he exclaimed, "What a blessing has she been to me! What would have been my misery if she had not had that magnanimity of spirit, joined to her tenderness, as never to have desired me to do a base thing to save my life! What a week I should have passed, if she had been crying on me to turn informer and to be a Lord Howard! God has granted me a signal providence in giving me such a wife, where there was birth, fortune, great understanding, great religion, and great kindness to me; but her carriage in this extremity is beyond all! It is a great comfort to me to leave my children in the hands of such a mother; she has promised to take care of herself for their sake, and she will do it." He stopped, and his thoughts returned to his own situation: "What a change death must make in us! What new and wonderful scenes will open to the soul! I have heard how some who were born blind were struck when, by the couching of their cataracts, they saw; but what if the first thing they had seen had been the rising sun?" He wound his watch and gave it to Burnet, saying, "I have done with time, now eternity comes."

The next day, the 21st of July, Lady Russell was a widow, alone in her residence at Southampton House, with her three children, two daughters of nine and seven years, and a son of three.

VIII.

Lady Russell in Widowhood.

Upon opening the letters written by Lady Russell after this terrible blow, one cannot suppress his surprise to find that the first two from her hand are addressed, the one directly and the other indirectly, to Charles II., to the king who had refused her the life of her husband. She had immediately retired from London with her children for Woburn Abbey, the seat of her father-in-law, the Earl of Bedford. Here she wrote to her uncle, John Russell, Colonel of the First Regiment of Foot:

"Apology, dear uncle, is not necessary to you for anything I do, nor is my discomposed mind fit to make any; but I want your assistance, so I ask it freely. You may remember, sir, that a very few days after my great and terrible calamity, the king sent me word he meant to take no advantage if anything was forfeited to him; but terms of law must be observed, so now the grant for the personal estate is done, and in my hands, I esteem it fit to make some compliment of acknowledgment to his majesty. To do this for me is the favor I beg of you; but I have writ the inclosed paper in such a manner that, if you judge it fit, you may, as you see cause, show it to the king, to let him see what thanks I desire should be made him. . . . It is not without reluctance I write to you myself, since nothing that is not very sad can come from me; and I do not love to cause trouble to the friends and relatives of my beloved and now blessed husband."

A report from the city soon reached Lady Russell in her retreat: so great a disturbance had been produced throughout the country by the publication of the paper which Lord Russell had given to the sheriff on the scaffold, that the Court had been induced to deny its authenticity. Lady Russell considered this an injurious attack upon the memory of her husband, and she hastened to write to the king:

"May it please your Majesty: I find my husband's enemies are not appeased with his blood, but still continue to misrepresent him to your majesty. It is a great addition to my sorrows to hear your majesty is prevailed upon to believe that the paper he delivered to the sheriff at his death was not his own. I can truly say, and am ready in the solemnest manner to attest, that [during his imprisonment*] I often heard him discourse the chiefest matters contained in that paper, in the same expressions he therein uses. I do, therefore, humbly beg your majesty would be so charitable to believe that he, who in all his life was observed to act with the greatest clearness and sincerity, would not at the point of death do so disingenuous and false a thing as to deliver for his own what was not properly and expressly so. I hope I have written nothing in this that will displease your majesty. If I have, I humbly beg of you to consider it as coming from a woman amazed with grief; and that you will pardon the daughter of a person who served your majesty's father in his greatest extremities, [and your majesty in your greatest posts,] and one that is not conscious of having ever done anything to offend

---

* The words included in the brackets are crossed out.

you [before.] I shall ever pray for your majesty's long life and happy reign."

It is a widow in despair; the fondly-devoted wife of a conspirator, executed a short time before on the scaffold for maintaining the right of resistance and the liberty of his country, who preserves and manifests so simply this profound monarchical respect, this susceptibility so gentle in its language, though so lofty in its tone. Days, months, and years flowed by; she remained the same—entirely absorbed, but not overwhelmed in one sentiment—concentrated in herself, and at the same time attentive, active, and even expansive to all interests around her. She had a confidential friend in Dr. Fitz-William, who was formerly her father's chaplain, and who was now rector of Cottenham and canon of Windsor. He was a man of deep piety, with a sympathetic heart and an elevated, fertile mind, who felt the tenderest interest for the noble daughter of his former patron, and he exerted himself to sustain, console, and advance her through all her trials toward God and her eternal salvation. Lady Russell opened her heart to him; to him she revealed all her inward conflicts, her paroxysms of grief, and her devotional self-conquests. I wish to present some of the most striking characteristics of this correspondence; not enough to fully reveal this great soul, but sufficient to make it understood in its rare and admirable union of fervor and good. sense, tenderness of heart, and firmness of mind which never neutralized each other. During her forty years of widowhood she belonged exclusively to the memory of her adored husband, yet continued active and attentive to all the relations, affections, duties, and it may almost be said, all the interests of life around her. Shortly after her affliction, Dr. Fitz-William had sent her some religious counsels and forms of prayer to assist her in her devotional exercises. She replied to him: "I need not tell you, good doctor, how little capable I have been of such an exercise as this.* You will soon find how unfit I am still for it, since my yet disordered thoughts can offer me no other than such words as express the deepest sorrows, and confused, as my yet amazed mind is. But such men as you, and particularly one so much my friend, will, I know, bear with my weakness, and compassionate my distress, as you have already done by your good letter and excellent prayer. You that knew us both, and how

* Her husband was executed, or rather murdered, July 21, 1683, we lived, must allow I have just cause to bewail my loss. I know it is common with others to lose a friend; but to have lived with such a one, it may be questioned how few can glory in the like happiness, so consequently lament the like loss. Who can but shrink at such a blow."

And some days later: "God, who knows our frames, will not expect that when we are weak we should be strong. This is much comfort under my deep dejections, which are surely increased by the subtle malice of that great enemy of souls, taking all advantages upon my present weakened and wasted spirits, assaulting with divers temptations, as, when I have in any measure overcome one kind, I find another in the room, as when I am less afflicted (as I before complained) then I find reflections troubling me, as omissions of some sort or other; that if either greater persuasions had been used, he had gone away; or some errors at the trial amended, or other applications made, he might have been acquitted, and so yet have been in the land of the living, (though I discharge not these things as faults upon myself, yet as aggravations to my sorrows.")

"Lord, let me understand the reason of these dark and wounding providences, that I sink not under the discouragements of my own thoughts! I know I have deserved my punishment, and will be silent under it; but yet secretly my heart mourns, too sadly I fear, and cannot be comforted, because I have not the dear companion and sharer of all my joys and sorrows. I want him to talk with, to walk with, to eat and sleep with: all these things are irksome to me now; the day unwelcome, and the night so too. . . . When I see my children before me, I remember the pleasure he took in them; this makes my heart shrink. . . . O, if I did steadfastly believe, I could not be dejected; for I will not injure myself to say I offer my mind any inferior consolation to supply this loss. No; I most willingly renounce this world—this vexatious, troublesome world—in which I have no other business but to rid my soul from sin, secure by faith and a good conscience, my eternal interests; with patience and courage bear my eminent misfortunes, and ever hereafter be above the smiles and frowns of it; and when I have done the remnant of the work appointed me on earth, then joyfully wait for the heavenly perfection in God's good time, when, by his infinite mercy, I may be accounted worthy to enter into the same place of rest and repose where he is gone for whom only I grieve."

After having passed ten months in solitude and quiet, she felt the necessity of a change of scene. She wrote to Dr. Fitz-William on the 20th of April, 1684: "I am entertaining some thoughts of going to that now desolate place Stratton for a few days, where I must expect new amazing reflections at first, it being a place where I have lived in sweet and full content; considered the condition of others, and thought none deserved my envy; but I must pass no more such days on earth; however, places are indeed nothing. Where can I dwell that his figure is not present to me! Nor would I have it otherwise; so I resolve that shall be no bar, if it proves requisite for the better acquitting any obligation upon me." And five months after, the first of October of the same year: "I have resolved to try that desolate habitation of mine at

London this winter. The doctor agrees that it is the best place for my boy, and I have no argument to balance that, nor could take the resolution to see London till that was urged; but by God's permission I will try how I can endure that place, in thought a place of terror to me; but I know if sorrow had not another root, that will vanish in a few days."

She did not immediately execute this project, and six weeks after she wrote to the doctor: "I have, you find, sir, lingered out my time here; and I think none will wonder at it, that will reflect the place I am going to remove to was the scene of so much lasting sorrow to me, and where I acted so unsuccessful a part for the preservation of a life I could sure have laid down mine to have had continued. It was, doctor, an inestimable treasure I did lose, and with whom I had lived in the highest pitch of this world's felicity. But I must remember I have a better friend, a more abiding, whom I desire with an inflamed heart to know, not alone as good in a way of profit, but amiable in a way of excellency; then spiritual joy will grapple with earthly griefs, and so far overcome as to give some tranquillity to a mind so tossed to and fro, as mine has been with the evils of this life; yet I have but the experience of short moments of this desirable temper, and fear to have fewer when I first come to that desolate habitation and place, where so many several passions will assault me; but having so many months mourned the substance, I think (by God's assistance) the shadows will not sink me."

God, indeed, came to her aid, and though she sometimes sunk into abysses of grief, she never failed to rise from them; the well-balanced firmness of her mind and the profound piety of her heart enabling her conscientiously to avoid all exaggeration of sentiment in the appreciation of her lot. The two following letters are admirable proofs. The first is dated Woburn, October 11, 1685:

"Who can praise God's mercies more than wretched I, that he has not cut me off in anger, who have taken his chastisement so heavily, not weighing his mercies in the midst of judgments! The stroke was of the fiercest, sure; but had I not then a reasonable ground to hope that what I loved as I did my own soul, was raised from a prison to a throne? Was I not enabled to shut up my own sorrows that I increased not his sufferings by seeing mine? How were my sinking spirits supported by the early compassions of excellent and wise Christians, without ceasing, admonishing me of my duty, instructing, reproving, comforting me! He has spared me hitherto the children of so excellent a friend, giving them hopeful understandings, and yet very tractable and sweet dispositions; spared my life in usefulness I trust to them; and being I am to linger in a world I can no more delight in, has given me a freedom from bodily pain to a degree I almost never knew; not so much as a strong fit of the headache have I felt since that miserable time, who used to be tormented with it very frequently. This calls for praises my dead heart is not exercised in, but I hope this is my infirmity; I bewail it. He that took our nature, and felt our infirmities, knows the weakness of my person, and the sharpness of my sorrows."

The second is dated July 11, 1686:

"I know, sir, I am very tedious; and

if it be impertinent, I know also you will take it as if it were not so. Now I take this freedom scarce with anybody else; but it is a great indulgence to myself, and I am very certain you are pleased I should use it. I find it most especially useful on the return of these my saddest days, when dismal and yet astonishing remembrances crowd fastest into my mind. It is true, we can (you are sure) bear the occasions of grief without being sunk and drowned in those passions; but to bear them without a murmuring heart then is the task, and in failing there lies the sin. O, Lord, lay it not to the charge of thy weak servant; but make me cheerfully thankful that I had such a friend to lose, and contented that he has had dismission from his attendance here, (an expression you use I am much pleased with.) When my time comes that I shall have mine, I know not how it will find me then; but I am sure it is my best reviving thought now; when I am plunged in multitudes of wild and sad thoughts, I recover and recollect a little time will end this life, and begin a better that shall never end, and where we shall discover the reasons and ends of all those seeming severe providences we have known. Thus I seem to long for the last day, and yet it is possible if sickness, or any other forerunner of our dissolution were present, I would defer it if I could, so deceitful are our hearts, or so weak is our faith. But I think, one may argue again, that God has wisely implanted in our nature a shrinking at the approach of a separation, and that may make us content, if not desire a delay. If it were not so implanted there, many would not endure the evils of life, that now do it, though they are taught duty that obliges us thereto."

She wrote sometimes with unreserved confidence, as to her sentiments, to those persons who had rendered important services or manifested genuine sympathy in her affliction. Lord Halifax, among others, had interceded with the king at the time of Lord Russell's execution for permission to have his family escutcheon placed over the door of his house, as would have been done if he had died a natural death. This favor he had obtained with great difficulty. He had continued the most affectionate relations with Lady Russell, and had doubtless at some time attempted to offer her some of those cold consolations which can only satisfy souls that do not need to be consoled, for she wrote to him:

"My Lord, for my part, I think the man a very indifferent reasoner, who to do well must take with indifference whatever happens to him. It is very fine to say, Why should we complain that is taken back which was but lent us, and lent us but for a time, we know; and so on. They are the receipts of philosophers I have no reverence for, as I have not for anything which is unnatural. It is insincere. And I dare say they did dissemble, and felt what they would not own. I know I cannot dispute with Almighty power; but yet if my delight is gone, I must needs be sorry it is taken away, according to the measure it made me glad.

"The Christian religion only, believe me, my lord, has a power to make the spirit easy under great calamity; nothing less than the hope of being again made happy can satisfy the mind: I am sure I owe more to it than I could have done to the world, if all the glories of it had been offered me, or to be disposed by me."

God reserved for her efficacious but bitter consolations the fearful prospect of new afflictions. Her son, scarcely four years of age, fell dangerously sick, and recovered only at the last extremity. "God has been pitiful to my small grace," she wrote to Dr. Fitz-William, "and removed a threatened blow, which must have quickened my sorrows, if not added to them—the loss of my poor boy. He has been ill, and God has let me see the folly of my imaginations, which made me apt to conclude I had nothing left, the deprivation of which could be matter of much anguish, or its possession of any considerable refreshment. I have felt the falseness of the first notion, for I know not how to part, with tolerable ease, from the little creature. I desire to do so of the second, and that my thankfulness for the real blessing of these children may refresh my laboring, wearied mind, with some joy and satisfaction, at least in my endeavors to do that part toward them their most dear and tender father would not have omitted; and which, if successful, though early made unfortunate, may conduce to their happiness for the time to come here and hereafter. When I have done this piece of duty to my best friend and them, how gladly would I lie down by that beloved dust I lately went to visit, (that is, the case that holds it.) It is a satisfaction to me you did not disapprove of what I did in it, as some do that it seems have heard of it, though I never mentioned it to any besides yourself.

"Doctor, I had considered, I went not to seek the living among the dead; I knew I should not see him any more wherever I went, and had made a covenant with myself not to break out in unreasonable, fruitless passion, but quicken my contemplation whither the nobler part was fled, to a country afar off, where no earthly power bears any sway, nor can put an end to a happy society; there I would willingly be, but we must not limit our time: I hope to wait without impatience."

She waited long for that blessed reunion so sincerely desired, though she was not deluded by her grief regarding the weakness of our nature in that respect. While awaiting it as the years flowed on, she treated herself in her grief as we are obliged to submit to a chronic disease with which we learn to live when it is found that there is no hope of a cure. Notwithstanding the void in her heart, her life was active; she was constantly employed without ever ceasing to feel her great loss. The education of her children, their advancement, her domestic affairs, the interests and prosperity of her neighbors, were all the objects of her assiduous cares. "I am delighted," wrote Burnet, "that you devote so much of your time to your children, that they have no need of a governess," and her daughters never had any other. She was careful that her habitual sadness should not disturb the happiness which belonged to their age. "The poor children," she wrote, "are well pleased to be a little while in a new place, ignorant of how much better it has been, both to me and them; yet I thought I found Rachael not insensible, and I could not but be content with it in my mind. Those whose age can afford them any remembrance should, methinks, have some solemn thoughts for so irreparable a loss to themselves and family;

though after that I would cherish a cheerful temper in them with all the industry I can; for sure we please our Maker best when we take all his providences with a cheerful spirit."

For her father-in-law, the Earl of Bedford, she entertained the most grateful affection. When he lost his wife she gave up her plans for traveling, and remained with him. "I would not choose," she said, "to leave a good man under a new oppression of sorrow, who has been and is so very tender to me."

It was to Lady Russell that the different members of the family turned in all the important circumstances which concerned them. At the request of the parties she made the arrangements for the marriage of her brother-in-law, Edward Russell, with a daughter of Lord Gainsborough, father-in-law of her sister Elizabeth. It was well known that her counsel would be judicious, and that her approval would have great influence. "I have done it," she said on one of these occasions, "though I wish she had made choice of any other person than myself, who desiring to know the world no more, am utterly unfitted for the management of anything in it, but must, as I can, engage in such necessary offices to my children as I cannot be dispensed from, nor desire to be, since it is an eternal obligation upon me, to the memory of a husband, to whom, and his, I have dedicated the few and sad remainder of my days in this vale of misery and trouble."

The event, so important to so tender a mother, arrived earlier than she had expected. Her daughter Rachael was only fourteen years of age when Lord Cavendish, Earl of Devonshire, asked her in marriage for his eldest son, who was but sixteen. This nobleman had been the most intimate and devoted friend of Lord Russell; he had even urged him to change clothes and escape from the Tower, while he remained a prisoner in his place, which was unhesitatingly refused by Lord Russell. Deeply touched by the sentiment which had dictated the proposition, and sensible of the honor of the alliance, Lady Russell accepted the offer with frank gratification. "I trust," she wrote to Dr. Fitzwilliam, "if I perfect this great work, my careful endeavors will prosper; only the Almighty knows what the event shall be; but sure it is a glimmering of light I did not look for in my dark day. I do often repeat in my thoughts, the children of the just shall be blessed; I am persuaded their father was such; and if my heart deceive me not, I intend the being so, and humbly bless God for it."

The settlements of the respective fortunes were difficult to arrange; the most elevated sentiments are sometimes united with obstinate and exacting demands. "I have a well-bred lord to deal with," said Lady Russell, "yet inflexible if the point is not to his advantage." The interviews and discussions necessitated by the business negotiations wearied her. "I am forced to be with a great many lawyers, which is very troublesome at this time to me, who would fain be delivered from them, conclude my affair, and so put some period to that inroad methinks I make in my intended manner of living the rest of my days on earth. But I hope my duty shall always prevail above the strongest inclination I have. I believe to assist my yet helpless children is my business; which makes me take many dinners abroad, and do of that nature many things, the performance of which is hard enough to a heavy and weary mind; but yet I bless God I do it."

The final arrangements were completed at last, and on the 21st of June, 1688, her daughter married Lord Cavendish. The young couple departed immediately to travel upon the continent.

Judging from appearances, it might be supposed that Lady Russell's life was spent in strict privacy with her sad but precious remembrances, her religious meditations, and her family cares and duties. But it was not so. Hers was not a mind of much variety or fertility, and she was not spontaneously inclined to seek or find subjects of excitement or interest without. Left to herself, and to the routine of ordinary life, she would perhaps have remained a stranger to the great questions and events of her time; but she entered into them naturally, through sympathy with her husband, and she was capable of comprehending and enjoying whatever was elevated. She remained as faithful to the cause of Lord Russell in her retirement as she was to his memory; and she was constantly interested in the same questions of religious and political liberty which would have been the subjects of their common solicitude and private discussion if he had remained with her. The Revocation of the Edict of Nantes called forth not only her deepest sympathy for the suffering Protestants, but some original and profound moral reflections. "I will take your advice," she wrote to Dr. Fitz-William, "and vie my state with others, and begin with him in the highest prosperity, as himself thinks, the king of a miserable people; but truly the most miserable himself, by debasing as he does the dignity of human nature; and though for secret ends of Providence he is suffered to make those poor creatures drink deep of a most bitter cup, yet the dregs are surely reserved for himself. What a judgment is it upon an aspiring mind, when perhaps half the world knows not God, nor confesses the name of Christ as a Saviour, nor the beauty of virtue, which almost all the world has in derision, that it should not excite him to a reformation of faith and manners; but with such a rage turn his power to extirpate a people that own the Gospel for their law and rule!"

All that transpired in her own country interested her yet more deeply: the trial and death of Algernon Sidney; the accession of James II., the progress of his tyranny; the insurrection of Monmouth, and the sufferings endured by many of her friends in the cause which was so dear to her, revived the most cruel remembrances in her heart. At times she drew unexpected consolation from these misfortunes. "The new scenes of each day," she writes to a friend, "make me often conclude myself very void of temper and reason, that I still shed tears of sorrow and not of joy, that so good a man is landed safe on the happy shore of a blessed eternity. Doubtless he is at rest, though I find none without him, so true a partner he was in all my joys and griefs. I trust the Almighty will pass by this my infirmity; I speak it in respect to the world, from whose enticing delights I can now be better weaned."

But these efforts of a devoted nature could not long appease real anxieties and real troubles. The religious and political situation of England became every day darker; and Lady Russell, who was passionately attached to her country, was increasingly pained and alarmed for her children, for the nation, and for the future of that cause for which Lord Russell had perished.

IX.

Her Latter Years.

The Revolution of 1688 drew Lady Russell from her life of monotonous grief. After five years of widowhood and painful sympathy with the defeat of the political party with which she was identified she suddenly found herself triumphant though under the burden of her grief. The two months between the landing of the Prince of Orange and the final flight of King James she spent at Woburn. Though far from the noise and excitements of London, with her father-in-law and her children, she was well informed of all that transpired, and followed the course of events with the restrained ardor of an intelligent soul, knowing the uncertainty of great enterprises, but placing with a religious trust her country and her family in the hands of God. Her letters show that she eagerly read the articles published on both sides in the journals of the day, and that she was familiar with the details of incidents both in the city and in the Court. Anxious for the fullest information, when she learned that the Prince of Orange and Dr. Burnet had arrived at Salisbury she wrote to the latter by a special messenger: "The bearer leaves Woburn with no other errand than to carry this paper and return, charged, I hope, with such good reports as every good soul wishes, for curiosity may be too eager, and therefore not to be justified; but now it is unavoidable. I do not ask you should satisfy any part of it, further than you can in six lines; but I would see something of your handwriting upon English ground, and not read in print only the labor of your brain."

Toward the termination of these events Lady Russell went with the Earl of Bedford to spend some days in London; it was probably at that time that King James asked the assistance of the Duke of Bedford; the venerable nobleman replied, "Sire, I had a son who might have been now the support of your majesty!" Lady Russell was almost a witness of the decisive scenes which placed William III. upon the throne. "Those who have lived longest," she wrote to Dr. Fitz-William, "and therefore seen the most change, can scarce believe it is more than a dream; yet it is indeed real, and so amazing a reality of mercy, as ought to melt and ravish our hearts into subjection and resignation to Him who is the dispenser of all providences."

Though Lady Russell had maintained no relations with the Prince of Orange, they were neither unknown nor indifferent to each other. William knew too well the value of Lord Russell's name in England, and the respect paid to his widow, not to be careful to recognize them in advance. When he sent his embassador Dykenelt to London in 1687, he gave him orders to visit Lady Russell and express to her in his name his profound esteem and great respect for her. I transcribe verbatim the recital given of this interview from the hand of Lady Russell, written the 24th of March, 1687. "I have received," she said, "a visit from Mr. Dykenelt, the Dutch embassador. He spoke in French to this effect: To condole on the part of the Prince and Princess of Orange my terrible misfortunes, of which they had a very feeling sense, and continued still to have so; and as my loss was very great, so they believed my sorrow still was such; that for my person in particular, as also my own family and that I had married into, they had great respect and value, and should always readily take all occasions to show it; that it would be a great pleasure to them, if it would give any ease to my thoughts, to take the assurance that if ever it should come to be in their power, there was nothing I could ask that they should not find a content in granting. That for the re-establishing of my son, what I should at any time see reason to ask would be done in as full and ample a manner as was possible; that he did not deliver this message in a private capacity, but as a public minister. Then again he enlarged his compliment, giving me the content to tell me the high thoughts the prince always had, and still preserved, of my excellent lord; that his highness had never accused his intentions even at the time of his suffering, and had considered and lamented it as a great blow to the best interest of England, the Protestant religion; that he had frequently before heard the prince take occasion to speak of him, and that he ever did it as of one he had the best thoughts of one could have of a man.

"And he said (with protestations that he did not do so to make an agreeable compliment to me) that he found the very same justice given to his memory here, and that so universal, that even those who pretended no partiality to his person or actings yet bore a reverence to his name; all allowing him that integrity, honor, courage, and zeal to his country, to the highest degree a man can be charged with, and in this age, perhaps singular to himself; and, he added, all this completed with great piety. Words to this effect (as near as my memory can carry it) he several times repeated, and gave (as he termed it) one remarkable instance, at what rate such who were not his professed friends esteemed his loss. It was this, that dining at Mr. Skelton's (then the king of England's resident in Holland) immediately after the news had come thither of my lord's sufferings, and Mr. Dycknelt taking notice of what had passed, and in such a manner as was most proper for him to do to Mr. Skelton, Mr. Skelton sat silent when he named the Lord Essex; but that upon my Lord Russell's name he replied upon it, 'The king has indeed taken the life of one man; but he has lost a thousand, or thousands, by it.' Mr. Dycknelt then added, 'This I know to be the very sense of so many that I should not have repeated it but for this reason, I do it because Mr. Skelton said it.'"

When William III. was proclaimed king, he hastened to confirm with emphasis the words which two years before his minister had addressed to Lady Russell. On the 13th of February, 1689, after accepting in the morning the crown which Parliament had conferred upon them, King William and Queen Mary held in the evening their first reception at Whitehall. Lady Russell was not present—a stranger to all worldly pomps, she neither left her retirement nor laid aside her mourning; but her daughter, Lady Cavendish, appeared at Court with her mother-in-law, the Countess of Devonshire. "I have kissed the queen's hand, and the king's also," she wrote the next day to her cousin, Jane Allington. "There was a world of bonfires, and candles almost in every house, which looked extremely pretty. The king applies himself mightily to business, and is wonderfully admired for his great wisdom and prudence in ordering all things. He is a man of no presence, but looks very homely at first sight; but if one looks long on him, he has something in his face both wise and good. But as for the queen, she is really altogether very handsome; her face is very agreeable, and her shape and motions extremely graceful and fine. She is tall, but not so tall as the last queen. Her room was mighty full of company, as you may guess."

Political acts very quickly followed these royal courtesies. A bill was adopted in Parliament, stigmatizing the condemnation of Lord Russell as murder. One of the articles declared that "the bill was presented at the request of the Earl of

Bedford and Lady Russell." Sir Thomas Clarges demanded that these words should be omitted. "The justice of the nation," said he, "is of more importance than the wishes of any private person; this bill is not granted as a favor; all England is interested in it." This was the second act which William signed after his coronation. Soon after, in order to manifest his favor at the same time to the two families, united by domestic ties as well as by political sentiments, he conferred the title of Duke upon the Earls of Bedford and Devonshire. The letters patent to the new Duke of Bedford declared that "among the reasons for conferring this honor, this was not the least, that he was the father to Lord Russell, the ornament of his age, whose great merits it was not enough to transmit to posterity, but they (the king and queen) were willing to record them in their royal patent, to remain in the family as a monument consecrated to his consummate virtue, whose name could never be forgot so long as men preserved any esteem for sanctity of manners, greatness of mind, and a love to their country, constant even to death."

Domestic enjoyments came to Lady Russell at the same time with these political honors and reparations. She married her second daughter, Catherine, to Lord Ross, eldest son of the Duke of Rutland; and her son, Lord Tavistock, only fifteen years of age, to Miss Howland, a rich heiress of Surrey County. In none of these arrangements, however, were her decisions precipitate, or influenced only by considerations of rank and fortune. She hesitated some time before consenting to her daughter's alliance with the family of the Duke of Rutland on account of some scruples concerning a divorce; and she refused a richer marriage for her son than the one he finally contracted. The brilliancy of these alliances and the family prosperity naturally attracted public attention; but no one appeared surprised or envious; the nation openly manifested its sympathy for the justice of God to virtue in affliction. The relatives and friends of the Russell, Cavendish, and Wriothesley families delighted in relating to Lady Russell in her retreat at Southampton House accounts of the gay festivals to which she remained a stranger. After her marriage with Lord Ross, her daughter Catherine was conducted by her husband to Belvoir, the family seat of her father-in-law, the Duke of Rutland. On this occasion Sir James Forbes, the same gentleman who ten years before had borne to the condemned Lord Russell the proposal of Lord Cavendish to take his place in prison, wrote to Lady Russell: "Lord Ross and Lady Ross's journey, and their reception at Belvoir, looked more like the progress of a king and queen through their country, than that of a bride and bridegroom going home to their father's house. At their first entry into Leicestershire they were received by the High Sheriff at the head of all the gentlemen of the county, who all paid their respects and complimented the lady bride at Harborough. She was attended next day to this place by the same gentlemen, and by thousands of other people, who came from all places of the country to see her, and to wish them both joy, even with huzzas and acclamations.

"As they drew near to Belvoir our train increased, with some coaches, and with fresh troops of aldermen and corporations, besides a great many clergymen, who presented the bride and bridegroom (for so they are still called) with verses upon their happy marriage."

While these aristocratic and popular festivals were detailed to Lady Russell, she received congratulations from her religious friends, which doubtless harmonized better with her frame of mind. "You have passed through very different scenes of life," wrote Burnet, who had now become Bishop of Salisbury. "God has reserved the best to the last. I do make it a standing part of my poor prayers twice a day, that as now your family is the greatest in its three branches that has been in England in our age, so that it may in every one of these answer those blessings by an exemplary holiness, and that both you and they may be public blessings to the age and nation."

At the time of her son's marriage she received a proposition for him as singular as it was flattering. A general re-election was preparing for the House of Commons; the Duke of Shrewsbury, grand Seneschal of the Crown, and Lord Somers, Keeper of the Seal, begged Lady Russell to allow her son, notwithstanding his youth, (he was but fifteen,) to be presented as a candidate at the elections for Middlesex County. "I made all the objections to their lordships," Sir James Forbes wrote to her on this occasion, "that I think the Duke of Bedford or your ladyship can make, yet they were still of one opinion, that it is your interest and for the honor of the family that he should stand at present; and being joined with Sir John Worsename, a very honest man, who is recommended by my Lord Keeper, they doubt not but they will carry it with a high hand, and thereby keep out two notorious tories, which can never be done otherwise. When I told their lordships that my Lord Tavistock was soon going to Cambridge, and afterward to travel for two or three years, the Duke of Shrewsbury answered that they would not hinder anything of that design; for he needed not to appear but once at the election, when he would be attended by several thousands of gentlemen, and other persons on horseback out of town, and the charges would be but little or nothing; and the Duke of Shrewsbury bid me tell your ladyship that if you did consent he should stand, which he doubted not but you would, since it was on so good an account, that then they must have leave to set him up for that day only by the name of Lord Russell, which would bring ten thousand more on his side, if there be so many freeholders in the county."

What temptations for the maternal love and pride of Lady Russell!

X.
Her Last Days.

She did not yield to these temptations; she had two great forces to defend her; her piety and her grief. On the occasion of the titles and honors conferred upon the Russell family, "I would have assisted," she said, "to my power for the procuring thereof, but for any sensible joy at these outward things I feel none." She declined with a good sense full of modesty, the premature triumph that politics offered to her son. Inclosing the letter of Sir James Forbes to her brother-in-law, Lord Edward Russell, she requested his lordship to consult the Duke of Shrewsbury on the proposal, and expressed her doubt whether the latter had maturely considered the subject. She reminds him of the serious interruption which the education of her son must suffer by his election to Parliament, an interruption which she feared might be irreparable in the future.

Maternal wisdom triumphed over party interests, and instead of presenting her son at the elections of Middlesex County, Lord Tavistock went to complete his education at Oxford, "where our young nobility," she wrote to Dr. Fitz-William, "should pass some of their time; it has been for many years neglected."

In the simplest incidents of private life she displayed the same correct judgment, uprightness, and moral delicacy; admonished and guarded by these against the prejudices, thoughtlessness, carelessness, and haughtiness too common in aristocratic old age. Before deciding to give her daughter Catherine to the son of the Duke of Rutland, she asks the latter "whether your lordship does not think we owe this to the young couple, that they should see one another a little more than they have done (and so at least guess at each other's humor) before we venture to make them, as I hope they shall be, a happy couple?"

Some years later she had at her disposal two ecclesiastical benefices, in virtue of her right of patronage. She wrote to one of her friends, Sir Robert Worsley, "I find both places well disposed to receive Mr. Swayne. I hope he is worthy of the gift, and believe you think him so. If you should know anything why he is not, though as a friend you might wish he were the incumbent, yet I am persuaded that in a just regard to the weight of the matter, and to me who ask it from you, if you know any visible reason that he is not a proper person for such a preferment, that you will caution me in it; for I profess to you, sir, I think the care of so many souls is a weighty charge; and I have been willing to take time to consider whose hands I put these into. I can, with all my scruples, make no exception to Mr. Swayne."

So much virtue and wisdom, seen through such various trials, in the midst of prosperity as well as in the bitterest adversity, gave her a consideration and almost a moral authority with the people as well as with the Court which few women have obtained who have made much more noise in the world. After their elevation to the throne, as before, King William and Queen Mary continued to manifest the same interest, and the same regard for her wishes. At the time of the Revolution, when the formal adhesion of the Princess Anne was necessary for the coronation of the Prince of Orange, Lady Churchill, afterward Duchess of Marlborough, and confidant of the princess, would not advise her to take this step "till I had consulted," she says, "with several persons of undisputed wisdom and integrity, and particularly with Lady Russell of Southampton House, and Dr. Tillotson, afterward Archbishop of Canterbury." Tillotson hesitated some time before accepting the archbishopric from the hand of a king whose title was not yet recognized by a part of the English Church. Lady Russell influenced his final decision. Consulted by him on several occasions, and informed of the earnest requests made to him by the king, after having examined and discussed the doctor's scruples, she wrote to him, "The time seems to be come that you must put anew in practice that submission you have so powerfully both tried yourself and instructed others to. . . . Sir, I believe you would be as much a common good as you can; consider how few of ability and integrity this age produces. Pray do not turn this matter too much in your head; when one has once turned it every way, you know that more does but perplex, and one never sees the clearer for it."

With her more intimate friend, Dr. Fitz-William, she was not equally successful. Either from real scruples of conscience or from timidity in hearing the opinion of a part of his Church, he refused to take the oath and resigned his benefice. Lady Russell endeavored to dissuade him from this resolution, though equally conscientious with himself. She wrote to him, "And all this is the acceptation of a word which I never heard two declare the meaning of but they differed in their sense of it. You say you could have taken it in the sense some worthy men have done. Why will you be more worthy than those men? It is supererogation. When I began to write in this paper I meant not one word of all I have said on this subject; but I know, good doctor, you will take it right; accept well of my good meaning toward you, and excuse my defects. I pretend not to argue; but where my wishes are earnest, I speak without reserve; sometimes by surprise; but take it as it is."

This difference of opinion did not, however, change their pious relations to each other for a moment.

On all occasions, and with all her connections, after the triumph of her cause, and amid her own successes, Lady Russell was as judicious, as far from all elation, as liberal in mind and heart, as she had been firm and constant in her reverses. In but a single instance have I found her exacting and peremptory. She had warmly interested herself to have a distinguished young man of her acquaintance made one of the king's Council. Her *protegé* was William Cowper, who afterward became Earl Cowper, and in the reign of George I., Lord Chancellor. The request met many strong objections; a dispensation of age was necessary. Lady Russell insisted, first with Lord Halifax, and afterward with Sir H. Pollexfeu, Attorney-General of the Crown. Her letter to the latter closes with this sentence: " I undertake very few things, and therefore do very little good to people; but I do not love to be balked when I thought my end compassed." It is the only case of pretension I have discovered in this upright and modest nature; justified, it is true, by the merit for which she plead, but yet bearing a slight impress of pride and exaction.

Lady Russell really knew herself better, and judged herself more harshly than the most rigid moralist could have done. After her death an unfinished paper was found, written in the trembling hand of age, in which under a form of prayer she reviews the events of her life, confesses her errors and sins, and implores pardon of God with that anxious humility which is a distinctive feature of Christian virtue. I find this passage: "Vanity cleaves to me, I fear, O Lord, in all I say, in all I do. In all I suffer I am not enduring to slights or neglects, am subject to envy the good parts of others, even as to worldly gifts; failing in my duty to my superiors; apt to be soon angry with and without cause too often, and by it may have grieved those that desired to please me, or provoked others to sin by my rash anger; not ready to own any advantage I may have received by good advice or example; not well satisfied if I have not all the respect I expected, even from my superiors. Such is the pride of my heart."

I would not judge Lady Russell as severely as she judges herself; but in this accusation of pride and exaction she touches the weak part of her nature, and displays as much penetration as sincerity.

As she grew old, surrounded with so much respect, illustrious in her mourning, happy in her country and in her family, a gradual and beautiful transformation was produced in her character. The same remembrances and the same regrets were equally present, but they were no longer accompanied with the same anguish. Time, habit, weariness, and that detachment from self which age produces in superior natures, softened the sharpness of her grief without destroying it. Her affection for her children, her solicitude for their virtue and happiness, held a larger place in her heart, and left less room for the intense and bitter regrets which belonged to her own part. Religion, its anxieties, duties, exercises, and devotions, constantly occupied her thoughts and became her habitual practice. In a word, she possessed Christian calmness and resignation, and though her love was ever consecrated to the same object, she was more submissive to God, confiding in the eternal future, and more occupied in securing it than impatient of obtaining it.

These sentiments are apparent in a long letter which she wrote to her children in 1691, before the marriage of her second daughter and son; it gives them, in the utmost freedom, the counsels, examples, and exhortations of her faith and tenderness. "My dear children," she says to them, "I write this upon the 21st of July, a day of sad remembrances to me, it being that whereon your excellent father was taken from us with much severity, to my lasting sorrow and your loss. I have not yet omitted on this day (but when prevented by sickness) to humble and afflict myself under the mighty hand of God, pouring out my soul before him in prayer and fasting.

"As, first to testify my humiliation for all my sins, for my having offended God in so many and so frequent breaches of my baptismal vow, my sacrament vows, and all those vows I have at any other time made of a better and more strict obedience to all his holy commandments.

"I recollect as well as I can what they have been, and make my resolutions to do better for the time to come; and, as a help to my memory, I did now look over some notes I had by me of some former examination; at other times I have done it by considering all the passages of my life which I have by me, noted in a paper after the same manner I set yours down, and gave it you when you first received the sacrament."

She describes to her children her daily practice of rigid self-examination, her habitual prayers, and reading both in the Holy Scriptures and in works of religious instruction and edification. "I take my paper and consider what I have been most faulty in this week, as wandering in prayer, or negligent in reading, or passionate, or envious, or what else. I set it down (in as few words as I can) at the foot of my dayly notes for that week; and so that is an abridgment for the whole week. Saturday morning begins the next week; and upon the first Friday in every month, or the last, just before I use my confession, I look upon my notes and consider the actions of the whole month, if nothing but common has happened the less examination will suffice; only I take care so to recollect as may represent anything that is remarkable or great, either to be matter of sorrow or thanksgiving, (for other things a general care is proportionable,) and make my resolutions accordingly. This gets on a habit of a constant watchfulness; and at sacrament times, or at any other time that I would examine myself, I find it a great help to read this. It saves much time in looking back, and one's thoughts are less distracted, and makes our lives more easy to us when we see how we live from one sacrament to another. And this makes religion easy, and the mind quiet and full of tranquillity; and though it may seem a hard task at first, yet a little use makes it none, though if it be—for flesh and blood is apt to draw back at the times of devotion, and especially at such like exercise—yet if it help us to live more innocently, and to state things more reverently and usefully between God and our souls, no pains is too much, but on the contrary, doing this will upon trial (I speak it by experience) be found less pains to such as mean to be serious in religion.

"My child, believe your mother; there is nothing now in this world can touch me very sorely but my children's concerns, (bating religion,) and although I love your bodies but too well, yet if my heart deceive me not, 'tis as nothing in comparison of your more precious souls. When I have the least jealousy that any of you have ill inclinations, or not so good as I would gladly have them, or fear that you tread though never so little out of the right path, O how it pierces my soul in fear and anguish for yours! If you love or bear any respect for the memory of your father, do not endanger a separation from him and me in the next life; but infinitely above all other argument is this, that we should not be ungrateful to that God that made us and preserves us; made us be born into this world that we might be capable of a life to all eternity, where innocence and happiness last forever; to this place of joy and bliss this is our passage, and is to some more rugged than 'tis to others, for wise ends, by Providence hid from us now; but when we shall have put off these tabernacles of clay our clarified spirits shall then understand, and admire, adore, and love the wisdom and power and love of God to his creatures. How lovely will the beauty of providence be to us then! though now that we see but the dark side of the cloud, 'tis often very black and gloomy to us.

"And now, my dear child, I have but little more to add, except to put you in mind to remember this life at longest is but short, and how short none can tell; but if you live, crosses will come and pleasures wear away. Strive to get gospel evidence of your being a child of God, and having a title to the promises of eternal life. 'Tis this, believe me, my dear child, 'tis the witness of an honest and good life in the day of trouble and distress, no refreshment then but in a well-founded hope to enjoy a happy eternity; and to what a degree, that calms and sweetens the most bitter sorrows, is inconceivable by such as have not felt it, as I bless God I have ever since I could get over the astonishment of so great and so sudden a blow. When I am cast down with some sad reflections of what I have lost, I do as soon as I can sum my thoughts to consider that in a short time I shall leave this world and go to a place, where I shall see Him who died for me; I shall then know much of the reason of all these providences we do now so little understand and think so severe. I shall meet all my pious friends again, and what a joy will it be to feel continual springs of pleasure, a perpetual and entire quiet in our own minds; no sickness, no bad appetite, no passion shall remain in us, but a constant joy in being extremely good; and the sense that this will be perpetual must add a freshness to that fullness of joy which could not be entire if we did not foresee it would be endless. O blessed, longed-for day!

"O my beloved children, take care we meet again. Do but experience the pleasure of a well-spent life, and the pure delights of meditating on the future state of eternity; that you may do so, and love it, to my last breath you will have the prayers of a truly loving mother. Consider, my dear, that all the innocent delights of life you may take, and have no anxiety of mind with them; but if they shut out religious thoughts and performances, and devour and take up all our time, then indeed we sin, and conscience will sting at some time or other, and be a sore remembrancer, and check us in our gayety; but be devout and regular in your duties to God, then heaven will be secure, and pleasures innocent."

I do not believe that a sweeter and more solemn exhortation can be found, in which tender anxiety is better united with fervent piety. Lady Russell needed to preserve all her fortitude; her trials were not yet ended. Ten years from the day when these fervent words were addressed to her children she was by the bedside of her son, the Duke of Bedford, who had been suddenly seized with small-pox. The young duchess and his children had been removed from fear of contagion; the mother remained alone to sustain the courage and receive the last words of her expiring child. He died. "Alas! my dear Lord Galway," Lady Russell wrote some days after to her cousin, Henry de Ruvigny, "my thoughts are yet all disorder, confusion, and amazement; and I think I am very incapable of saying or doing what I should. I did not know the greatness of my love to his person till I could see it no more. When nature, who will be mistress, has in some measure, with time, relieved herself, then, and not till then, I trust the Goodness, which hath no bounds, and whose power is irresistible, will assist me by his grace to rest contented with what his unerring providence has appointed and permitted. And I shall feel ease in this contemplation, that there was nothing uncomfortable in his death but the losing him. His God was, I verily believe, ever in his thoughts. Toward his last hours he called upon him, and complained he could not pray his prayers. To what I answered, he said he wished for more time to make up his accounts with God.

Then, with remembrance to his sisters, and telling me how good and kind his wife had been to him, and that he should have been glad to have expressed himself to her, said something to me of my double kindness to his wife, and so died away. There seemed no reluctance to leave this world, he was patient and easy the whole time, and I believe knew his danger, but loth to grieve those by him, he delayed what he might have said. But why all this? The decree is past. I do not ask your prayers; I know you offer them with sincerity to our Almighty God for your afflicted kinswoman."*

Six months had scarcely passed when another terrible blow struck Lady Russell; her second daughter, the Duchess

---

* The young Duke of Bedford left several children at his death, among others two sons, from whom have descended the present Duke of Bedford and his brother Lord John Russell.

of Rutland, died in childbed. Of her three children, her eldest daughter, the Duchess of Devonshire, alone remained to her, and she was on the eve of her confinement. Resolved to conceal the death of her sister, the mother replied to the pressing questions of her daughter, "I have seen your sister out of her bed to-day." She had seen her in her coffin.

Nearly twenty years before this last calamity Lady Russell had been in danger of losing her eyesight; the operation for cataract, though successfully performed, had left her with but a difficult and precarious use of her eyes. The few letters which remain of this sad period of her life are deeply sorrowful but calm, as from a captive awaiting deliverance after seeing all whom she loved go forth from their common prison. May 28th, 1716, she wrote to Lord Galway, who had also been afflicted in his dearest affections, "I also pray to God to fortify your spirit under every trial; till eternity swallows all our troubles, all our sorrows, all our disappointments, and all our pains in this life. The longest, how short to eternity!"

In September, 1723, Lady Russell was alone in her London residence, Southampton House, where she had lived with her father and husband, and during her widowhood. On the 26th of the same month her grand-daughter, Lady Rachael Morgan, wrote from Chatsworth to her brother, Sir James Cavendish, "The bad account we have received of Grandmamma Russell has put us into great disorder and hurry. Mamma has left us and gone to London." "I believe she has stopped the letters on the road, for none have come here to-day, so that we are still in suspense. I should be very glad that mamma should get to town time enough to see her, because it might be some satisfaction to both, and I hear grandmamma asked for her."

God granted this last satisfaction to the mother and daughter. Lady Russell expired the 29th of September, 1723. The British Gazetteer announced her death on the 5th of October, as follows: "The Right Honorable the Lady Russell, relict of Lord Russell, died on Sunday morning last, at five o'clock, at Southampton House, aged eighty-six, and her corpse is to be carried to Chenies, in Buckinghamshire, to be interred with that of her lord." The last words of Lord Russell to Burnet were at last fulfilled for his wife, as well as for himself; she had done with time, she had entered into eternity.

I have taken a profound interest in sketching this character, so pure in affection, so constant in grief, always great and always humble in her greatness, faithful and devoted with the same ardor to her sentiments and duties, in joy and in sadness, in triumph and in adversity. Our own times are tainted with a deplorable evil; it is the belief that passion must be without restraint. Intense love, perfect devotion, and all the fervent, exalted emotions which master the soul, can exist only, according to this depraved creed, when freed from moral laws and social conventionalities. In its eyes all rule is a yoke which paralyzes; all submission, degrading servitude; and all warmth is extinguished unless it flames into a consuming fire. Unfortunately a graver evil still is, that all this does not arise from paroxysms of feverish temperament and the power of exuberant force; it has its source in perverse doctrines, in the rejection of all law, of all faith, of all superhuman existence, in the idolatry of man, putting himself in the place of God, himself alone his only pleasure and his only will. To this evil is added another not less deplorable. Man not only worships himself alone, but he worships himself only in masses, in which everything is confounded. He both hates and envies all above the common level. All superiority, all individual greatness, of whatever kind or name, appears to these insane and weak minds a crime and oppression toward that chaos of indistinct and ephemeral being which they call humanity. They are triumphant when any odious example of vice or crime is detected in the upper ranks of society. They boldly employ these lamentable revelations of the more elevated circles as an argument against all social distinctions. They wish to have it believed that these are the general manners, the natural consequences of high birth or condition, regardless of the title or foundation upon which it is raised. When one has been assailed with these base doctrines, and the shameful passions to which they give birth, and has felt the disgust, and in some measure the peril which spring from them, it is a profound pleasure to find some of those noble natures which give a decisive denial to such assumptions. I respect collective humanity as much as I admire and love its glorified image of what is noble and pure, personified and elevated with visible features, and bearing a proper name. Lady Russell affords the soul this beautiful and genuine joy. She is a great Christian lady. She is a stranger to me no longer; her sentiments touch me, her fate absorbs me as if she were living before my eyes; I believe when she departed from this life, filled as it was with such bitter trials to her, she entered into that world, which is vailed from our eyes until God shall call us to it, to receive with her beloved husband the recompense of her virtues and her griefs.

THE END.

www.ingramcontent.com/pod-product-compliance
Lightning Source LLC
Chambersburg PA
CBHW030309170426
43202CB00009B/935